Landfall

Landfall

Poems

Keki N. Daruwalla

SPEAKING TIGER BOOKS LLP
125-A, Ground Floor, Shahpur Jat
New Delhi – 110049

First published in hardback by Speaking Tiger Books 2023

Copyright © Keki N. Daruwalla 2023

ISBN: 978-93-5447-340-1
eISBN: 978-93-5447-341-8

10 9 8 7 6 5 4 3 2 1

Typeset by SŪRYA, New Delhi
Printed at Chaman Enterprises, New Delhi

All rights reserved.
No part of this publication may be reproduced, transmitted, or stored in a retrieval system, in any form or by any means, electronic, mechanical, photocopying, recording or otherwise, without the prior permission of the publisher.

This book is sold subject to the condition that it shall not, by way of trade or otherwise, be lent, resold, hired out, or otherwise circulated, without the publisher's prior consent, in any form of binding or cover other than that in which it is published.

'Now by a secret pathway we proceed...'

(From Canto X of Dante Alighieri's Inferno. *Translated by Rev. H.F. Cary.)*

CONTENTS

Night Train	11
Matheran	12
The Bakula	14
Snow Leopard	16
Night Fishing	17
Leaves	18
Ladakh Nocturne	19
Hope in Our Times	21
Leaf	22
On the Blue Jay God	23
Of Near Absolutes	25
If You Open Your Window	27

CYPRUS AND SALAMIS

Salamis	31
Houses	35
Night Sea	37

ALASKA POEMS

Notes on a Sanctuary	43
Winter Migration	45
Mother Bear	46

Conversing with a Bald Eagle	48
Why	51
The Architect Ruminates on the Wetlands	55
Shepherds Outside Agamemnon's Tomb	57

LANDFALL AT CANTO X

Prologue of Sorts	61
Soul-Voyage	64
Medieval Scholar Arrives at Canto X	65
Aftermath—the Return	69

BLACK DEATH SONNETS

Prologue	75
Black Death	77
Chalk	83
If There Were a Goddess of Peace	85
Of Neo-Godses	86
Interrogation of a Muslim	87
Hathras	88
Iceberg at Abu Dhabi	90
There Are Wars	91
The Sad City	92
We Knew	93
The Bindu and Raza	94
Halfway to the Minaret	95
Notations	97
Untitled	98

We Are Not Alone	99
Advice to Old Poets	101
Nirvana	102
The Minotaur Waits	103
Gallery Number 4, MoMA	104
Pankha	109

THE NIGHT ATTENDANT

The Night Attendant 1	113
The Night Attendant 2	114
The Night Attendant 3	115
The Night Attendant 4	116
The Night Attendant 5	117
She Said	118
Nothing Big	119
Goddess on the Grindstone	120

List of Illustrations   123

Night Train

All is black and opaque;
shadows that swirl past
are darker than spaces
between constellations.
When the night train moves
into the unseen fringe of dawn
it carries the dark with it.
Edge of light
shredding the edge of form.

Through the frost-white window
trees black-lit;
seeding of colour starts:
light bickers with mustard flower
over a tone of yellow,
a banyan philosophizes
over its hedge of prop roots
burrowing into the grass,
a gout-afflicted scarecrow
stretches its arms sideways,
a pond flowers white with herons.

Matheran

How come this summer when the heat
is incandescent, sky white, just a band of glare,
and birds, as they hood their eyes, hide in tree hollows,
I think of the rains in Matheran,
that forested hilltop dripping
with shadows and leeches?
Father never lived on this hill, no gene-memory took me there.
But he left me a book on Matheran with a haunting green cover
which has disappeared now (and so has father
and so his books, holding on to words in their faded lettering
on yellowing paper).
It was written by a nineteenth-century Englishman
who loved forgotten hills; the passage of the monsoons
had the splendour of Sheridan on Awadh
as he thrust his verbal rapiers into Hastings,
or Burke on his lament for Marie Antoinette.
Here was lightning whipping itself
on the rock-ramparts of the Ghats—
cosmic self-flagellation—and the thunder
snared by rock crevices, echoing and re-echoing
into the night. I see those words
disappear into my eyelids beyond recall.

How does a fitful glimmer
move into memory through words?
And how did that clamour
and electric damp disappear into dream?

The Bakula

(For Mariam Karim Ahlawat)

Half hidden by shrub, the mother fox
watched the Reynar play with a boy
who didn't know they were fox cubs.
And a pregnant neelgai walked
fearless on the empty mall,
as some stragglers reached for cameras, not guns.

The peacock with its plumes
quarried from a turquoise mine,
its call inlaid with metal, danced on the tar,
not knowing it wasn't supposed to.

Salt flats looked out for flamingoes who never came,
the mauve carnival of feather and down
did not descend on waiting eyes;
and the French lady
with the semi-Mesopotamian name
who had sailed down the Tigris
as her naming ceremony was underway,
looked out of the window and found
a bakula, with its aphrodisiac petals—
the tree which sends out its flowers only

when beautiful women rinse their mouths
with sweet wine and let go on the stem
which wears a tiara of black bees around it.

When all this was observed by someone
on his morning walk on the Andromeda Galaxy,
he called out to his beloved, 'Look down,
it's not such a bad planet after all.'

Snow Leopard

Time shed
its arthritic antlers
as it trundled off for a thousand years
without looking back at you.
The mountains you roam, snow leopard,
broke their backs over a million years;
razor-edged shale and shard
and an islanded tuft of grass
in the rubble tell a story.

Time, good raconteur,
puts its spyglass down in opaque country
as it talks to us about the snow that pelts
your eyes and slides down the curtain of your lashes,
even while you wait out
wind and cold coming from the sky
and you meditate on time
through the snow,
through the white curtain
that shrouds yak country
and marmot country
and mountain goat country.

Night Fishing

The night still, the boat unmoving and a call from a far-off rock as if from another sea; the line drops like the first look of love, not stirring the water, or perhaps stirring it. Is night a hermit, he thinks. Wet breeze and thought trouble the old man, and the catch—fish intricately mottled, belly a sliver of palpitating silver; thought troubles him, coral and molluscs static under a heaving sea, but his sea is not heaving, it is not frothing on the beach but kissing it, it is still, he thinks of the sea-floor, fish moving over shell and sand, and the mangrove forest guarding the coast, and he compares mangrove with the brain, mangrove as memory, sea as life sloshing around it, and slowly the head drops into a dream and the tremor on the line pulses away and he doesn't notice.

Leaves

Leaves renew themselves across branches and the years,
>meaning they are always there;
leaves renew themselves among barbet song
>and the early morning sun.
Who was that Greek philosopher who said
>the Earth,
it was never created, it was always there?
>So are leaves and babblers;
and at the year's evening, or vesper-time,
>as old poets called it,
the air itself turns yellow as twilight
>and the leaves underfoot
like a conquered people's language
>develop their own undertone
and slang till the final one-time crunch.

Ladakh Nocturne

The temple bell is still
and its heavy metal ring
that cleaves the sky at dawn
            is quiet,

quiet as the stars that lie still
in the unruffled pond.
Bird-dreams are also silent
as crow and mynah roost on the lone tree
in this grassless landscape.
Birds go back in time:
the dreams that flash like
magic-lantern slides across their eyes
are from the silent movie era.

The prayer drums that girdle this holy
conglomerate of stones
are one with the stillness of the night.
The Gompa is surprisingly stable
atop that rocky hill, which looks
like a cataract of boulders
           halted in descent.

The Sakyamuni inside in his lotus pose,
gold and nirvanic peace painted on his face,
is meditating on eternity,
even as a thick shawl of mist wraps itself
around the monastery, so that it looks
like a mound of incense smoking up
from the shale valley to the stars.

Hope in Our Times

(Written on New Year's Eve)

Night bulletins are rife with Rafale and Sabarimala
as bare-chested devotees keep the pot churning.
Here the cold's dense, heavy, as a watchman adds twigs
and dry bark to keep the chaff fires burning.
Hope and light, small-time thieves in the fog,
cling stealthily to something close to yearning;
and through a hole in the mist, suddenly
a barbet calls, 'The year is turning.'

Leaf

Leaf
    crinkled at the edge with gold dust;
leaf
    winter-bitten but not hard enough,
    the bite sparse with gold dust;
leaf
    this broken bit of a filament of light
    drift-falls past a moss-draped stone-slab,
    sidesteps an overground root
    that snakes through the grass;
leaf
    nudged by a moment now,
    nudged by an air current to a tuft
    of grass in the shade of the mother tree.

On the Blue Jay God

I started a novel
fifty years ago
called 'The Blue Jay God'
and dumped it.
It was about tribal lands I never
visited, tribes I never saw,
dressed in leaf and bark,
their lives wrapped in leaf and bark.
I couldn't decide if their women
wore clothes ablaze with colour,
if their demons were ostracized by black magic
or demons had thrown out black incantations
and pins stuck in statuettes.
I couldn't decide which of the two was worse,
or why they couldn't live or die in peace,
or why we couldn't just let them be.

But I got a train ticket
for imagination to go there,
talk to their coffee-coloured women
dressed in their smiles,
a metal band across their wrists
instead of bangles;
their curiosity about my fountain pen amusing:
'Words should be spoken, isn't it,

why write them?'
The whole thing would have been a breeze,
writing those pages which memory misplaced.
Time is unforgiving.
Why did I abandon the novel
about people who had lived with dusk
but had never seen a streetlight?

Of Near Absolutes

1

The coffin-lid tells the nail:
We could be meeting soon.

I reflect on absolutes
and absolutes can mislead

more than uncertain mumblings and half truths
uncertain about facts loaded on the other half.

Why should the echo of thunder be considered true
as it rummages in the dome of the sky

and gathers ions and iron filings floating in the air
then explodes and frightens the dog under the bed?

An absolute doesn't climb or move (does it think?);
It guards the gates, guards the river-ford.

2

Childhood said to memory: We should part now,
what we know of each other is dubious, we've lost ourselves.

Myth said to reason: Climb down,
come to my well and drink;

Forest to flute: You are driving away the spirits,
pipe down or I'll disinherit you.

Wind, unruly wind, says to flapping canvas:
I'll unfasten your tent pegs and fly away with you.

If You Open Your Window

If you open your window
>to the dark—
and they evade you,
>the constellations,
as they drift and dodge your vision,
>and the night owl hoots,
'You've missed them, the lamp lights
>above,' while other birds,
comatose in their dreams, turn restless
>by the hoots,
distracted by the owl's entry into space
>and non-space of dream;
and the sky looks like language
>as it winnows words
and scatters the unused ones
>on the floor of the night
and words glow like embers and slowly dim,
>while a reminiscence
perched precariously on memory's edge
>blinks and moves
into fadeout—you wonder why you opened
>the window at all.

CYPRUS AND SALAMIS

Salamis

(For Stephanos Stephanides)

The poet of Cyprus,
island poet, sold on sea breeze and memory,
poetry oscillating like gentle tide—
shore-wards, sea-wards—
memory moving between childhood and amnesia,
his village overrun by Turks, his island torn in half,
said to me, 'Why don't you write a poem on Salamis?'
I came dreaming of Xerxes, but the Salamis
I looked for was in Hellas, not sea-girt Cyprus.

He took me to the Armenian; when in trouble
go to Armenians, good people, let me tell you.
She was Ruth Kasheshian, forty years in Cyprus
amidst the alien corn, educating islanders
on the Levant: 'Can't sink in the Dead Sea;
you can't sink in a sack of salt, guys.'
'You want to write poems on Salamis,
and need history books?
Take this,' and like a hand-grenade she threw
Seferis at me. I had read Euripides,
bleak guy, nonbeliever like me,
who wrote, I remember from college,
'Tears, libations futile flow
to divert from their purposed ire

the powers whose altars know no fire.'
Shame on me, that turned out to be
from Aeschylus' *Agamemnon* as I
went over some of the tragedies again.

I have things against Euripides.
He wrote 'Helen' and turned her chaste.
What is wrong with passion?
She felt a Trojan arm around her girdle
and fell for him, what's wrong with
headlong love, which translates as passion
which translates as sex?
Dionysus and Apollo,
trudging along our dented psyche.

When stumped, look for an exit hatch—
IMAGINATION—finest invention
to counter lack of learning.
The sun has opened its doors—
dawn and the upland of Salamis
wake to the roar, and the eyes of the city
open to the sun's gold raiment splashed
in the sea, eyelids half-dropping against
the assault of colour stronger than
the shimmer of light ricocheting
from Byzantine bronze in monasteries.
Shade the cornea, beautiful women of Cyprus!
Eyes are windows to the soul,
to love and passion, shade the windows.

Don't approach Salamis
as a ruin, a burial mask,
meet it as we encounter life,
traverse it like a living lane—
dog resting in shadows,
hawker hollering to housewife,
goat calling to its lagging kid
slowing down to drop its black pellets
on uneven cobbles,
an old man ambling into nowhere.

Salamis lived safe and smiling between
the black tiger-stripes of history.
I want to say good things about Salamis,
I would smear the ruins with myrrh,
lacquer the Amphitheatre
with legend, imbue a protagonist
with a Pavarotti voice.

Twenty-seven hundred years ago
Assyrians came to Salamis.
They were kind, asked for tribute and got it
and kept the spear on the saddle.

I almost call them compassionate people
against the gradient of the Old Testament.

I am now between
Mediterranean and the Middle East,
so is the Armenian Ruth,
who knows of God's curse on Tyre
(add Sidon as collateral).
Tyre was rivalling Jerusalem, such hubris!
She knows about Mamluks,
and the fate of the library of Alexandria
at the hands of history's two pin-ups,
Caesar and Caliph Omar.

The morass
of in-betweens has to end; poetry
between shores and receding seas,
stone and memory,
Euripides and Seferis,
Homer's Helen and the chaste one;
and Salamis
between the Assyrian and the Turk.

Houses

'The houses I had they took away from me. The times happened to be unpropitious.'—George Seferis

The trouble with houses is doors:
doors to memory.

Why do recollections, as they travel
like wind over icebergs, trouble him—
the genealogy of lanes,
an acacia tree flowering on a bend,
a pocket-sized church
which the Queen of Romania loved?

The pull of the walls is tense,
such tension doesn't break;
you withdraw from the years
but yearning never subsides;
it is wider in expanse, acreage,
stronger than limestone and mortar.
It takes in the years lived there,
ghost voice, echo and roar of the sea
buried in the walls.

Shadows scuttle along the walls
till memory turns opaque
like spyglass hazing
with salt spray from the sea.
If the house had flown on wings
he would not wrestle with empty space.
But how could he wrestle with the years?

Night Sea

The night sea is a philosopher,
it is soft in the head, speaks to itself.

The night sea is a truth-seeker,
rumbles within itself to find the truth.

Each wave is the night sea entire, when
it climbs, its foam-line hangs on top, and moves
into timelessness, moment as meditation,
transcendent, still.

The night sea is a bowl, has bragging rights,
it knows it is as large as the vault of the sky.

The night sea is the night sea,
it is a different being.

Argosies on the night seas are perfumed,
incense trees from Pant to Hatshepsut are still fragrant,

perfume shimmies out from cedar-wood boxes
that hold on to the frankincense within.

The night sea is a purifier,
its music rinses the soul clean.

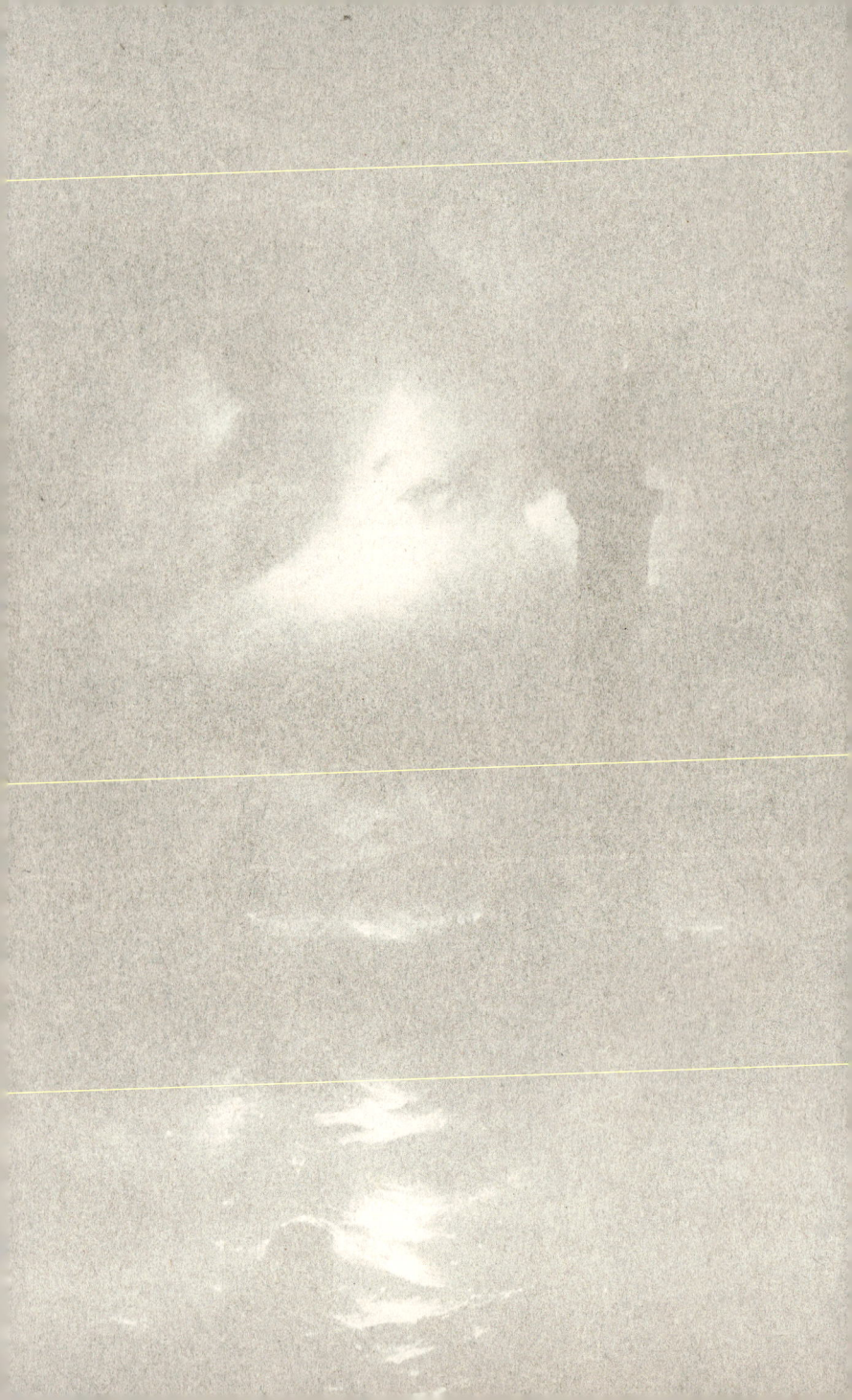

ALASKA POEMS

Notes on a Sanctuary

1

Merlin falcon, Falco columbarius, Lady Hawk, you've so many names. Precociously decadent medieval ladies used you for hunting skylarks! But your good days are over. You are as vulnerable as Parsis, thinning away despite your talons and those low-flying speed-bursts as you go after songbirds and turn the shoreline red. Worse, your eggshells are thinning too.

There's no way out for your kind; seems skylarks will trill again.

2

Predator and prey rise together. How does the lynx know that this is a good snow-hare year, six hundred per square mile? Mother lynx knows, keeps her ears to the ground, and begets more kittens.

3

Good friend beaver, keeper of my lodge, chief engineer of the dam, you don't know positive from negative, secular from spiritual, or the binaries of heresy and faith, of Commies and the RSS, the jet-setters and the Vedic inter-planetary voyagers with map directions and notations in Sanskrit. But you know your killers, fox, lynx and even bear. If death is chasing you, you'd better be quick, beaver.

Thank god you made it. What of your pursuer when he fails? Loss, dross, waste, he puffs and sleeps through nights with hunger folded in his arms like a beloved.

4

This six-million-acre sanctuary astounds me, confounds me; size and scale leave me with a bit of a hangover—you can walk three thousand miles without hitting a road. Shock-fall. I leave the ground, dust my trousers and holler, 'This park is for telescopes.' That black dot on the mountain, they tell me, is a bear. When it doesn't move, they say it is a black rock. The white spots are Dall sheep, they don't move either. The sun breaks through, comes down like a waterfall of light, and a caribou on its ridge walk decides to show off—who wouldn't with that thicket of antlers sprouting from its head?

Winter Migration

When early winter migrates to the lower tundra,
Dall sheep lead the way, their white coats silhouetted
against rust-coloured rocks. The bull caribou move out
of the dwarf birch and follow with their
vanguard of antlers, licking at the stubs of lichen
crinkling on the bark. Lichen and leaf, touched with red
only a week ago, have greyed, turned scabrous white.
Wolves have no choice, they follow.
But bear and squirrel and marmot are not
going to leave this musk ox country;
they dig, cold-cower—winter den will cloak their bodies
as they huddle into the long sleep that awaits them.
The bear will wake up if a warm spell moves
into the valley, but the marmot on her scree slopes
will freeze, even the brain turning to ice, and when she
wakes up with the thaw she'll shiver with the cold she lay with
for half a year, her tremor lasting hours, till she moves
around for the first signs of moss.

Overhead the white-winged crossbill and the Arctic tern
contemplate when to move to other skies.

The Arctic tern prepares for its
ten-thousand-mile flight to the Antarctic, six months
one pole and six on another, the planet too small for her.

Mother Bear

Our mothers are great in their own way,
but there is this Alaskan bear named Sky
(though very much of the earth, of snow and ice-fall,
smelly den and rock-and-rubble hill),
the way she handles her cubs leaves me dazed.
Pregnancy and hibernal sleep came together last fall,
and as free-of-ice water shoots through the valley
with the first thaw wind, she moves out with her cubs,
stripped of her fat and lean, takes a look
at the resurrected world, grass green again
and the sharp green cones of spruce and cedar;
lumbers towards grass and berry,
tests the rapids, anxious for her wobbling young,
takes the plunge and crosses over, hauling her cubs
till she meets the river which has gentled
and flattened itself for the salmon to spawn.
There are bears bigger than her here,
and hungrier—males, always hungry,
murder set like stones in their eyes,
paw and talon itching for her cubs;
she has to scare them, fight them off
and growl 'Over my dead body'
and scream swear words in searing grizzly language.

Salmon waters at last, and she jumps
on scuttling salmon and scurrying brook,
crashes with her paws till she nabs the fish
and tears half of it off and throws it to her young.

Conversing with a Bald Eagle

Landscape lush with conifer,
sky pewter grey,
sinew and soul in meditation,
the bald eagle sits on a lagoon rock-wall
at the sea's edge.

Her nest on the cedar
is not a brain fever bird's nest
intricate and weave-perfect,
but bristles with sticks,
a Neolithic artifact.
Her other sits on a cedar branch,
takes short flights and changes perch;
males can be restless.

Eagle, you have sat statuesque for an hour now.
I know your foot is taloned,
your beak hooked and yellow,
your sight keen—could spot a magpie
half a mile off, though at the moment
your eyes are the colour of rain.
Do you ever suffer from insomnia, bleed with anxiety
about your future and your next morsel?

I'd like to be with you for a day,
watch you run your beak through your brown feathers,
watch you angle around an alder thicket looking for mice, hare,
disassemble a stubborn lobster from its shell;
watch you climb that unseen ladder to the skies.

The guide tells me that you moult between three and five.
Born with a brown head, your scalp turns to snow
when you are five. You mate for life
and if he dies you stay single—
'like your Hindu widows'.
(I don't bother to tell her that widowers
can also walk in single file.)

The guide also says you are a raptor.
I don't believe her, you are not a goshawk
or a sparrow-hawk.
I can't see a songbird's throat, a magpie's leg
or a pheasant's copper feathers
on your dining table.

You don't know that all this land
was ice a million years ago;
that your ancestors could still smell ice in the first millennium.
But you know time,
You know that at eleven
the trawler will come and discard its fish trash;

and you wait, meditate
possibly mumble grace before your bits-of-fish
and shucked oyster meal.

I think of you as a hermit,
brown and snow-crested,
rainwater eyes awaiting the trawler.

Why

Why are we driving in this rain,
why are we driving in the day-dark
with the sky coming down on us
        with its wet
and its premonitions of sleet?
It is so cold-dark that conifers on the flanks
        turn to shadows.
Where exactly are we going? The headlights drag us;
what happens when the battery runs out
and the headlights dim?
Why are we driving in this rain?

We zip through rail crossings
but how many crossings will we pass
    and how long will the world—
with its own headlights streaming on the tar-wet—
        let us through?

I remember silos and harvesters in the fields
        as we motored on once.
Can still imagine bushels unloaded
and wheat and barley going down metal flues;
but now a smear covers all that, and the past itself,

as the sun of memory goes down
like the harvest went down the silo, grain by grain.
Why are we driving in this rain?

There's a divining bowl out there
but when the diviner looks into it
    the water has turned ice.
'Where's the future,' he asks, 'if the water is ice?
We can't wait for the thaw,
    for the thaw
is hidden from my eyes.

Hours before noon and the dark slides down
turning the side-glass black.
Metal cold, and glass cold, and we drive on.
Darkness drizzles down with the rain.
Are we moving to the North Pole?
What's so special about the Pole
that compass needles and metal hearts are drawn to it?
Is a half continent of iron buried there
    that drags us on torn tyres and bleeding knees?

If the seas turn ice, why move towards the seas?

The Architect Ruminates on the Wetlands

He hasn't got anything done today,
he's in a daze at this dust-and-amber moment.
His eyes smart at the surface glaze of the blueprints, paper
crackling like parchment or a shoulder shorn away.
At his office window twilight gravels through the dust
as he adjusts his lamp and re-adjusts it,
the lamp-light angles in on blueprints,
he skips over quotations from professional tree-fellers
(we don't call them lumberjacks here)
but each time he eyes them
he hears the sliced echo of a whine from an electric saw.

He pats his pay cheque.
His boss who has bought this sprawling acreage
of wetlands has hired attorneys, a black-gowned wall
against unknown forest laws.
'The lawyering will take care of the courts for twenty years,' he laughs,
a Cuban cigar barrelling out of his mouth.

He loves the wetlands, squelch and suck of mud-ooze,
shrike and marsh harrier, black drongo and speckled eagle owl,
waters filmed with algae,
a heron undecided where to land—
on algae, or water or strips of land within the water?

He remembers the shoots as a young boy with his father,
remembers how his father put his hand on the barrel
and lowered his gun
when a blue bull exploded from a clump
of thorn and saw-grass; remembers how they spotted pug marks
and backtracked, and the feral unease of the moment.
At night his imagination would reel in films—
rhinos sloshing in water, wild dogs loping in.

Memory sultry with nostalgia one has to lay off.
Now his job is to build a township here,
no trouble at the office, which he locks up and drives home.

Shepherds Outside Agamemnon's Tomb

One day they came in cars, more numerous
than a goat's udders or a bitch's litter,
went round our cave and snapped, 'Get out!'
'Hey man, you haven't heard us, give us a minute,
just one measly minute, will you?' 'Out!'

We'd been moving out with sheep each single dawn,
though in the winters light itself held back
(cold got to our knees) and we lazed a bit,
and let the bars of mist disappear from the hills
before stirring out, though sheep turned
impatient and sprayed the cave-floor with pellets.
'You lived here, and your wretched forefathers,
for seven hundred years,' they screamed,
the men in suits. How do we tell them that
time means nothing to us—just day and night
chasing each other like birth and death,
thirst and water, hunger and bread.

The men in suits said, 'This was Agamemnon's tomb,
tallest on the planet till some forlorn lighthouse,
its half-lit head a-swirl with night mist,
dwarfed it, or a Naiad's statue perhaps,
or one to a king's mistress.' We asked, 'Why did he need such
    a tall

building to live in death?' 'None of your bloody business!
And your fires blackened great paintings on the walls,
paintings of Troy, the fleet of warships
and the wooden horse,
your blasted fires turned them to soot.'

'How would lamb and infant survive
in the cavernous cold?' we asked.
The men in suits shouted, 'Out!'
So we moved, not in search of pasture
but a cave.

LANDFALL AT CANTO X*

---

*The poem was sparked off by two assertions in Canto X of Dante's 'Inferno', the first part of his epic poem *Divine Comedy* (completed in 1321): (a) According to Joel 3:2, the valley between Mount of Olives and Jerusalem will be the place where the Last Judgement will take place, and the dead will reclaim their bodies. There is a reference to this in Canto X, lines 10-12. (b) Lines 107-108 of the canto—after the Last Judgement, time will not exist.

Prologue of Sorts

It was a sad day, hashish I had imbibed,
also drinks, woke up from the trance bloody late;
the half blind lord waited at my bedside.

'Don't get into a dither, had your drink spiked.'
The fellow never left things to fate.
I faced up to what was coming—blight.

I knew his troubles, he was in the Arab's fist,
there was no room to wriggle. His Arab friend
was worse off—happens to alchemists.

If I were in this trade, I would have sold
from counterfeit crinkled chronicles
fake secrets copied from some fake scrolls

dug out from long-forgotten wells in Sinai.
Have no idea what these metals do
in their consanguineous union with each other, I

spot the Lord at his hookah, opium sprayed on coals;
a whiff of saffron I could sniff, and dolefully
I looked at last night's wine-and-arrack bowls.

The Arab trooped in, felled me with a hug
and roared while looking at me soulfully:
'You'll be our saviour.' I was truly bugged.

'You have Jinns in you, they can be a curse,
can also make you rise like oil on fire,
ascend to heaven, past purgatory or worse.'

What was this owner of furnaces and herds
that left horse shit in his courtyards trying to say?
I abandoned the claptrap of my dismal verse

and asked, 'O owner of deserts and oases,
what do you want me to do, I am shaky still
from last night's grog. What is the basis

of yapping on about purgatory, heaven and things
we know nuts about? These philosophers talk of
music of the spheres, do Mars and Saturn sing

as they circle Earth?' He stopped me, I saw fear
in his eyes: 'The Day of Judgement is upon us,
you don't know—the world, you and I will disappear.

Qayamat is descending, ledgers will be out.
Alchemy cheats both metals and morals.
Judgement Day will be an absolute rout.

Qayamat—how we sinners will roast and burn, O!'—
with hand on heart—'Before we die, and wine-skins dry,
I want something from the Inferno.'

He whispered in wizard-speech something I heard
or misheard. Like drops from a choked stream, a spell,
by-passing belief, language, the sacred word.

What's a word but to fly on, ah beatitude!
But how do I get there, up or down?
Was unsure of Hell's coordinates, latitude.

I sped on nonetheless, delaying would look rude.

Soul-Voyage

'Soul-voyage is the answer,' said the Chief Alchemist,
who had left the trade. 'Sorry to see you in this state,
heard tales about binges—couldn't resist?

You need time for equilibrium,' said the sage,
'for prayer, meditation, to change your fate
by a degree, a nail's growth. Stay at my hermitage

under arrest, and repent, no hashish or wine
to wet your lips or send your brain a-swirl.
If you improve, I'll grant you the word in time.

Mysticism means a flash of the divine;
unworthy ones may chance upon a pearl;
God's grace may evade me, yet descend upon swine.

Resume your scholarship, you were good with words
and conundrums once. Can't initiate you into alchemy;
if I hand you iron, it will turn to rust.'

My will was strong. Iron in my intent,
I would not ask for forgiveness; my credo:
If you want to be absolved, do not repent.

Medieval Scholar Arrives at Canto X

1

From the House of Agonies* this shout, I could tell,
'No bastinado for me, souls don't have feet.
You saints need guide books for your torture cell.

You hear shrieks, groans, laughter—noise thick as mud.
It's not fiends being tortured in some pit of hell.
Its do-gooders baying for sinner blood.'

I ran from the blasphemer and his sinful words,
made the sign of the cross, gesture that sat well!
The overhang lifted like a flock of birds.

I ran on fatigued, weary in mind,
side-stepping the horned vipers that filled the mire,
the farthest by far of its foetid kind

from heaven's high vertigo, the astral gyre
that made the head spin, as stars moved to their scripts,
scripts I can't read, never much of a trier.

---

*The House of Agonies: Canto X of 'Inferno' starts with a path between the Great Wall and the place where the tortured souls are suffering.

A voice rang out, 'The earth is mirrored in your face.'
That gave me hope, I looked for getaways:
a portal opened up—to nothingness and space.

2

I saw the faces of some migrant souls
mirroring their feet, torn to blistered shreds,
hunger clawing them from a hundred holes.

Were they of earth or the infernal regions?
Giddy, as ground circled, looked for something to hold
and still me, as stars swung round me in legions.

Such despair I felt, thought of the lined
dead looking up, the way the dead look
with stone eyes. What if they were still consigned

to coffins? Symbols there were to console despair
graffitied on the age, as terrors lurk.
Just put one horror behind me, I thought, and stared

at the heavens in that necrophilic calm,
looked out for grace, found a blaspheming Turk!
The heresiarchs lay there, mummified, embalmed.

They stumped me, muzzled, always suspect—
their egos floundering in philosophic murk,
where's the space for these sects and subsects?

3

Time enough to put the Gorgon* where she belongs,
her killer beam nullified—a quirk
of fate, fear multiplies a pile-up of wrongs.

Venice will dream of skeletons riding mares,†
while between Jerusalem and the Mount
of Olives—sun black as a sackcloth of hair—

the vale is getting readied for Judgement Day.
Winged angels descend with their trumpets
and the dead are warned there will be no delay.

Judgements signed and sealed, veneers peeled away,
no laxity now for saints or strumpets.
Torture pairs with justice, fire is here to stay.

And Time is held by the throat and told, 'Don't hound us.
Stop for good.' If Time stops, what happens to the spheres?
How will moments petrify, will lasting night surround us?

---

*Gorgon: Canto IX Lines 55-58 where Virgil asks Dante to shut his eyes in case Gorgon (Medusa) looks at him and kills him.

†Venice Dreams: During the Black Death, the bubonic plague, some terror-struck victims hallucinated that at night a skeleton would be seen, riding a horse.

4

Bloody hell, will moments get petrified?
And eternity, that staple of poets across the Hindu Kush,
traders in cosmic-speak—'verily', 'East', 'The infinite'?

No dealer in shrouds, sure I'd rather be
with the flame—tempered rich—horse silver-shod—
and spills from the cellars of Filippo Argenti.

Of no spot of earth or hell where light has died
will I be a part. Night is night but still in sleep
my brain whirls, songs forgotten lie at my side.

A halt to Time, not causing a furore!
The future lame, old and doddering
is ill at ease, itchy, insecure

as it meets the ages that have gone before.

Aftermath—the Return

'You haven't been seen, where did you go,
your pupils dilated, your eyes blood red?'
'I spent a dark month at the Inferno.

How the sinners are tortured, I am at a loss
to tell you, I sometimes side with sinners now.
I saw a fellow being boiled in sauce!

Saw angels cradling trumpets, like hail descending
with nets of liquid silver to catch sinner souls
which tried escaping like crabs. The world is ending!

"What if the sun stops its rounds and vision gropes
in black space?" I asked a man who wore long locks.
"What happens to helianthus and heliotrope?"

The guy thought I was insane!
The risen dead feared me more than the hail-fall
of avenging angels. I tried calming them in vain.

"The living world must be an absolute fucking mess
with specimens like you," Long Locks said, as he ran
while angels kept coming down; I felt both cursed and blessed

at the same time. But in a warped world, the tenses,
past and future, get muddled; had I taken
brief leave of the vigil of my senses?

Thought I heard him say my script moves right to left.
"Your half-blind lord can't read anymore.
So the two of us are sequestered and bereft."

My dream still wound thick like a ball of twine,
the Arab stepped in. 'Tell us, what made you visit Hell?
We just asked you for a Dante line

from the book, not from hell below or heavens above.'
They wished to move beyond symbols, flag and blazon,
                beyond falcon and dove.

I found it—'To think the universe was moved by love.'

BLACK DEATH SONNETS

Prologue

A clown comes on the stage.

The Devil never left Black Death in the foyer
to be discussed at length in devastating detail.
Cleverer than Satan and Iblis, those soul-sawyers,
the Devil could not let himself fail!

He checked out of Hilton, memory had him dismayed:
Didn't the hotel echo some rhymester of yore?
Yes of course, the guy who needed vision aids.

Having planted Brexit, the Devil planned an exit.
But how could he run, leaving Hilton behind?
Told the cashier, 'This place is truly gala.'

His task severe: bury memories of Black Death
in some catafalque, beyond the reach
of sonneteering bums like Daruwalla.

*

The boats don't keel as they unload their cargo
and Black Death, which has no nameplate yet,
clambers up Europe's back; the Fates, hard put to watch
its moves, have sin on their minds and redemption;
can cuirass, crown, a monk's cowl save a soul?

'They're all mashed up here, your fucking Highnesses
from Greek shithouses, naked corpses.
How would we gondoliers know who's who?'

A friar shouts, 'Wash the sickness into the sea,'
till he is scythed himself. Nations outlaw
coffin, cerements, shroud; or was it plague that did it?

The Cardinal hands over a year's hard labour
        for the crime.
The scribbler asks, 'What have I done, my Lord?'
'You dared write a sonnet without a rhyme!'

Black Death

1

The summons were from the Byzantium court,*
he was wanted there, the king's son was dead,
the advance guard of buboes had got to him.
'How did he take it?' he asked. The king's eyes bled,

the messenger answered. Isaac, coiner and scribe,
tried to address the king in that ornate hall
but hysteria ruled, courtiers screamed, 'The Tartars,
stricken with disease, threw plague across the wall,

they catapulted corpses into the city.'
The royal ribs withstood a shudder, 'Think of Kaffa,
that Genoese port, with terror, not with pity.

Leave witches alone, and their ghastly spells,
and keep the Jews away, they've suffered enough,
and no, they haven't put poison in our wells.'†

---

*King of Byzantium John VI Kantakou Zenos lost his son, aged thirteen, to the plague.

†Twelve ships docked at port Messina (Sicily) coming from the Black Sea and brought the plague. For Jews it was the biggest persecution before the Shoah. Those who were in debt of the Jews initiated the pogroms. The shilling the poem talks of is a coinage for the buboes in the armpit by a Welsh poet who lived in the times of the Black Death.

2

Reports from the sea crowd my dreams, winds seethe
with salt and fear; this could have been a jest
in the old days, a threat from rat and flea, but now
this line of rodents, themselves fleeing the pest,

frightens my court. Doctors tell us, the ones
in shining belts, with faces grey as sand,
that rats are the invading army of the plague,
buboes their night camps on our dying glands

which burn like cinders in the armpits, tough to view.
'Why have the heavens cursed us?' the victims shout,
those still left with some spark in their sinew.

'They did it,' the court says, 'beggar, witch, Jew
and migrants.' Were there minaret and dome
dusk-lit, they'd have blamed it on mosques aglow.

3

'How did we falter?' my queen asks, tongue timorous
as it moves in her just withered face.
'Were defilers abroad in our kingdom, blasphemers?
Did usurers have a free run of the market place?

Has your executioner taken leave of his axe?'
'He's dead, my lady, of the disease.' 'And during Lent

did the peasantry fast with us?' 'Some were lax,
but our kingdom's no longer a divine instrument.'

'Whose wrath have we incurred then, some scullion's
from Devil's kitchen, or an enraged spark divine?'
'Wife, too many heresies around, trackers of bad smells,
gluttons for good beef but guzzlers of bad wine.'

The plague moves on; for death it is harvest time.
Who dies tomorrow, rodents alone can tell.

4

Doubt doesn't clear the brain but corrodes.
    The future, will it float?
Or go down? The coming years are bands across the eyes.
No black sails flare with dark omens on the boats.
As the fleet from the Black Sea moves into Messina
with rodents draped in flea and flea bites that bleed,
what is the bird-liver reader doing here?
What on earth is there left to read?

Night, no Lord's Prayer comes in dreams; some hear tambourines!
Only the clatter of hooves on cobblestones,
as a skeleton rides a horse—must be quite a scene—

and women have seen fire in a dead man's bones
instead of marrow. The Queen
closes the door of dreams in sorrow.

5

The Cardinal from Venice

*[A pilgrim to Jerusalem, the Cardinal
drops by. Queen kisses his ring.
He offers his limp hand to me.
Sorry, I ain't gonna kiss no such thing!]*

'Death is dying,' he says, 'without absolution.
This nightlong traffic isn't going well.'
He shakes his locks: 'No penitence, no confession,
the spirit in agony hissing away to hell.'

'What of the stricken?' I ask. 'Shillings as they clink
in the armpit? Why so bogged down with the soul?
We need doctors more than priests, don't you think?'
My queen looks at me, her eyes burning coals.

He changes tack, 'The entire order will be upset,
the Holy Church itself could be facing blight.
It's an end to serfdom: footmen, scullions
will question authority—they'll ask for rights!'.

He waves his arms, 'When will all this be curbed?'
'There's no salve,' I answer, 'but Time is herb.'

Chalk

A girl who grew up in war-ravaged Poland in the 1940s—and who may have spent time in a concentration camp—was asked to draw 'home' on a blackboard while living in a residence for disturbed children in Warsaw in 1948. A photographer commissioned by UNICEF took this photograph of the girl with her drawing:

  her hair
     beribboned
  coat wrinkling in embarrassment
     at its sheen of velvet
    as she turns from the blackboard
     to stare at the counsellor who has asked
  her to draw
     'home',
  her eyes marked with new-found horror
    for her chalk had drawn
    a stack of barbed wire.

If There Were a Goddess of Peace

If there were a practising goddess of peace
        she would have celebrated
the judgement of the Five.
The trouble is, goddesses of peace
        are hard to find; gods
of war are a-plenty.
Is mythology also arraigned
against genuine peace
(as against the spurious one)
        and votes for dome batterers?
This leads to another question:
Does humanity deserve peace?
        (Must ask Derrida or Foucault,
            though I haven't read the buggers.)

Peace is not a scribble of words
dictated to a keypad in a musty room;
it is a cloud in summer
that keeps you from the sun.

The goddess of peace,
had there been one,
would have been disturbed
at the sight of a temple coming up
on the carcass of a mosque.

Of Neo-Godses

I read a poem
by Deborah Landau the other day
where she asked what the hell
was neo about neo-Nazis.
And I wondered what
was new about the
neo-fringe Savarkarites
and the neo-Godses
except that they could beat
you right up to the mortuary
and the police would serve them tea
and biscuits, ain't that the law?
They'd ask, 'Where are the guys
whom we bludgeoned?'
and they'd get the answer:
'One's in the autopsy room,
other's in the lock up.'

Interrogation of a Muslim
(After lines by Sridala Swami*)

I think of palaces in Junagadh,
gargoyles affixed
to gutters that vomit in the monsoons.

He is in khaki
(Brits coined the word from 'khaak', 'dust'),
a tilak long as a walking stick
bleeds on his forehead.
Prisoner squatting on the floor thinks:
His mouth is a gargoyle.

'I am not interested,' says Khaki,
'in your crimes against the state—
all that is recorded in discs, phone taps
and our extractions from mobile phones.

'I want your confession
of the crimes you thought
of committing.'

---

*From her poem 'Perforation': 'A temporary rain/ Wring out the confessions before they're put out to dry...'

Hathras

If, god forbid, you have a daughter in Uttar Pradesh,
let godlings be with you—village deities;
bell-god Ghantakaran on the way to Badri,
gods of cattle pens, high pasture spirits
glad to be near a goatherd's twig fire.
For it's 'high caste' hoodlums
who'll despoil her, break her neck,
wound her tongue, how else to silence her?
Doctors will fight shy of saying
she was raped, and an ADG,
that means an Additional Director General of Police,
will emphatically say she wasn't.

Past midnight she'll be cremated,
mother will not be shown her face,
sister won't see her ravaged body.
'Security reasons, enough fuel here for riots.'
Besides, other castes might say, 'So far so good,
a cobbler's family, a hide-flayer's daughter—
but hell's bells, tomorrow could be mine!'

Meanwhile, your village is barricaded
and some magistrate tells you,
'TV guys will vanish, and so will politicos,
and you'll have to settle with us, buster.'

The village will be lashed with 144.
Protesting leaders will be felled;
No one in the Cabinet will say boo, and Mr. Bisht
gets 20 FIRs filed against unknown people.
UP is not the right home for daughters.
Whether India is a better place,
we can discuss later.

Iceberg at Abu Dhabi

If you are at Jeddah, as I am, and it is night,
you can't believe it is night, for a million small suns
though not in the sky are at port,
blazing through glass—tube and globe.
Eyelids and cornea splinter and fall,
like insect wings after Indian rain,
as they gaze at the light-fall.
This isn't night, it's eye-tearing day,
the dazzle ferried from some region bordering night,
a billion lights burning to show ships coming from air
and screeching on hard land.

I am the baby iceberg torn from mother,
I broke away blessed by her, she seemed
off her rocker, shouting, 'Who knows when
we were transcribed into existence? Go.'
What the hell did she mean? Iceberg thinned,
water-roar broke the membranes around my ears
and I moved like voyagers who sailed the Caribbean
in the times when Jews were thrown out.

There Are Wars

I have lived with wars,
though they raged outside of me:
missed the great one by thirty years,
never saw rats in the trenches,
though I got immersed in poetry and the tanks
as they fenced with barbed wire.
I remember Enola Gay and Hiroshima
and a nameless man evaporating.

When peace descended, I lived with those
who wanted to tinker with it and shred it.

And I have lived with love.

And also with the green of grass, and birdcalls,
lived with poetry and light that rusts at dusk
and is alive at dawn,
and lived with my masks and those of others—
papier-mâché glued to wood.

Have lived with love and friends,
Lived with death and grieving.
What else is there to life?

The Sad City

('*Yeh sheher udas itna zyada toh nahin tha*' by Faiz Ahmed Faiz)

Though everyone didn't own a bar or plenty's horn,
This city was never so sad and woe-begone.

Two or three loonies roamed the by-lanes, forlorn,
But their garments were not hundred-patched or torn.

Love's wayfarer not spotting his love!
Simpleton he may be, he's not so lovelorn.

Fatigued momentarily, one day the eyelids closed
To sleep and never wake up—that was just not on.

The preacher and the drunk are both known to me,
The chasm between them is neither deep nor long.

This city was never so sad and woe-begone.

We Knew

the rooster would announce 'Night is over',
it took its time;
light would break through fog,
it took its time;
love and pine needles would light a spark,
they took their time;
she'd come after dusk darkened and windows lit up,
she took her time;
the year would end with a poem,
the year took its time;
the clinching line would come at the poem's end—
it sat at the door and chatted with the passing year,
and never came.

The Bindu and Raza

The bindu is amphibian, moving up
    the well of consciousness,
its hundred lives dredged from the ages
or from mystic or non-mystic states
in which the bindu was caught up.
The ages don't have a sure foothold themselves, are mixed up,
falling over each other as they grapple with this circular
    primordial bit from the past.
It changes colour, substance, scale and squats in front
and tells you gently to meditate: both are meditating,
        Bindu and Raza.
Now it has turned into a small circular bit
of granite, with its veins
running through the history of the planet;
it is not scabrous but is plain and rough
till the waters of the past and waters
of myth run over it and add lustre,
till bindu is Brahma
and all else is blotted out.

Halfway to the Minaret

'You have fever, father,
your knees stammer,

your spine becomes a bow
as you climb these corroded steps

in the pre-dawn haze; even stairs are confused,
they don't know if they're going up or down.

Birds, perched on the prayer-tower cupola,
don't fly away when you or your shadow approach.'

*

'You are my daughter,
the Muezzin's daughter,

the minaret's call is a daily electric shock
which you should have felt.

The curvature of my spine keeps my legs
steady; I know where my feet are taking me.

Birds don't fly away from me
since they think I'm speaking to the skies.'

*

'Father, no one listens to your call, the stairs
are muddle-headed, as old as you.

Time has eaten up the edges of the steps,
the stairs are debris and dust.'

*

When light grew loud and his dawn prayer
never rose like a white tendril from the incense stick

they looked for him
and found him slumped halfway to the minar.

Notations

Of a sudden
memory bled
winter got
into my bed

happened quick
as a finger's click
like light boards aircraft
and zooms off at dawn.

Solitude is one thing
gold never bought,
just live with that underground
train called thought.

Listen to me
wayward son:
winter and aloneness
they are one.

Untitled

In the swaddling dark
groping for dawn
on the left side of the bed

where the tall mirror has gone to sleep;
the sunlight cat hasn't diagonalled
it's soundless padding across the black-ink floor.

Sticky eyed, I wait for window glass
to get pecked and stirred into life
while a gaggle of distant car-horns

which have displaced the birds
find their muffled, mournful way through the dark
to tell me it is day.

We Are Not Alone

(Lao Tzu said this, or should've said it—that a poet must first educate his audience, only then write the poem. So here I start. I chanced upon an email which said that 'on October 19th, 2017, astronomers from the Haleakala Observatory in Hawaii announced that the Panoramic Survey telescope and Rapid Response System telescope had detected a strange object that had flown past earth twelve days earlier [on October 7th]. It was quickly realized that this visitor was an interstellar object, the first ever to be observed passing through our solar system'.

The object was named Oumuamua (pronounced Oo-moo-a-moo-a), which is Hawaiian for 'Scout', or 'Messenger from afar arriving first'. Initially there was confusion—was it a comet, an asteroid? Between 'optical, spectral and infrared data', its 'dimensions were inconsistent with any known celestial object'. It was the 'first sign of Intelligent Life Beyond Earth', as a recent book had 'prophesied'. It is cigar-shaped, 400 meters or so long, 40 meters broad, an intelligent object, red in colour. It has intelligence, says the email, it is a sentient being. For which, Lao Tzu says, use the pronoun 'he'.)

The intruder is here: It's a cigar, ET, an asteroid!
    A torpedo from the unknown to another void!

Skies mean nothing to Oumuamua, navigator skirting stars;
    He has over-spilled four sun-systems, traveller from far.

Time, distance don't confuse him, he confounds the two,
>   doesn't know life from death, doesn't care a jot who's who;

the speed so close to light, when the sun's
>   tentacled gravity reaches out for him

he dodges, shifts his mercurial trajectory,
>   a fawn-swivel before the cheetah-strike;

loves to gambol, like long-penned goat kid's
>   first day on the pasture; he delves

into verse, four-star clusters are quatrains for him,
>   Aldebaran and Sirius are ghazals in themselves.

Advice to Old Poets

Focus on bones,
not half rhymes, half tones,
Muse India's faded stars.

Your knees and hips
are warning blips
on hospital radars,

elegies and odes
(please burn your notes)
are no longer in flow'r.

Treat fractured iambs,
dislocated dithyrambs
as galaxies afar—

we can't reach them, buddies,
we fuddy-duddies.
Let's move towards the Bar.

Nirvana

The trouble with eternity is it has no locus.
The same goes for states of mind—
they have lookouts on imaginary towers
but where are the coordinates?
Nirvana falls in the same class—
it doesn't have sensors,
it can't even make a gesture.
Renunciation has all these, it has
something palpable to give up, even if
all that you renounce are the five or less senses.
Now how can that be, for renunciation leads to nirvana.
I'm gonna ask the Sakyamuni when I meet him next.
Like time, nirvana is also anti-material—
It must hate carrying this body around.

The Minotaur Waits

The minotaur is restless as he inhales
the unfamiliar smell of his own fear.
The stalker has a thread ball in one hand
and a sword in the other,
as they move through narrow darkness and bent walls,
their eyes burning with fevered visions.
Each thinks the other is on a killer prowl.

The minotaur waits, his two hooves pawing the stone-grit,
hammering out a spark or two
as he kicks up the black dust of the night.

He thinks time is on his side,
the night is his
and the whirlwind of walls that he moves in.

Has the labyrinth sprouted another passageway?
The thought bellows through the intricate
interstices of the angling walls.
Why is the fellow late?
He looks for the luminous dial
on his scruffy wrist, but the radium glow
has been blotted out, and the dial has gone
and the watch with it, for time itself, like a thief,
has slipped out.

Gallery Number 4, MoMA

1

Sidling past *Fission*
you wonder what these spheres
are doing in the gallery.

You look intently and find
the spheres collide
and the ones in the middle
get flattened into ellipses,
as if beaten by a baseball bat;

you haven't taken in all the horror
that broods over us all.
Spheres, geometrically sprayed, is that really art?
But then, what about the ellipses in the
fires of collision,
atoms collapsing as they meet and crash,
isn't that symbolic of nuclear physics?
Why must horror always be visual?
Why can't it come to us sieved through the mind?
I would rather see this
than some carrion-eye photograph
of blackened Nagasaki.

2

You move to the centre:
Gold Marilyn Monroe,
her hair yellow on top and black on the sides
(something to do with light and shadow perhaps?),
her lips more black than red
and the ultramarine shadow
daubed with a trowel on the eyelids.
Warhol could have done better, couldn't he?
I like the painting only for its
resemblance to the diva.
Then I notice the shadow of the jaw
circling her neck
like a black choker.

3

Andy redeems himself with the next one:
Double Elvis.
There he is, Elvis, in his jeans—or rather, *they* are,
for this is a double-image, just the edges blurred,
and a double image implies
something askew in our vision
as we rub our eyes.
Elvis is young here, not bloated,
and the pistol in his hands—their hands
(double image, don't forget)—
is just a black slash, but we know it's a pistol.

You don't need pistols painted there,
in art, the gesture should notify;
you don't need to show a bullet,
trajectory should suffice;
lethal arc of the projectile.

4

Jean Miró does this in his *Person
Throwing a Stone at a Bird* (1926).
You see just the leg of the thrower,
the outsized calf muscle on the grotesque foot.
Earlier I thought the bird had turned red
even before the stone-hit.
I was wrong.
First the contact and splash of blood
larger than the bird—
then bird-fall.
Meanwhile, the sky green,
earth desert-yellow,
the space where bird and stone meet
black as death.

5

Francis Bacon can stamp on your face,
thrust his brush and hackles in your eye.
He does so in his *Oil and Pastel on Linen*.
Painted in the late forties, his memories

still frying on the fires of war.
He tramps on the dark-suited politician's face
even though the fellow is half obscured
by the umbrella overhead.
That toothy grimace of his,
which starts almost from the forehead,
suggests brutality even
as your attention wanders
to the bright yellow boutonniere.
Behind him, above him
in flesh-pink and fat-white
stand the cow carcasses in cruciform.

Should art be that ferocious?
Secondly, doesn't a wrong politician
with or without a row of serried teeth
jutting out of his forehead
muddy a lot of pages
in the book of fate?

6

Canvas on floor, he flicks
enamel paint straight from the can and still
it flows into a rhythm, aided
by the painter's frenzy and stick and stiff brush.
What do you do with phenomena like that—
like Jackson Pollock's *One: Number 31, 1950,*
oil and enamel on unprimed canvas?

Just view it as you would a landscape
undulating in front of you.
The interlaced threads of paint wind around
a hundred luminous patches
and you could see a city here,
with its intense maze of traffic.
Just sit back and take it in, let the paint
sink into your eyes and thread its way
into your consciousness
like love, like longing.

Pankha

(For Jatin Das and his exhibition on fans.)

Shrivelled by the sun, drooping from cares,
the lover slouches into his mistress's house.
She draws water from the well for his ablutions,
then fans him, driving off irritation, anger, grouse.
The frown that sat on his cheek like a scar
leaves him, the furrows fly from his forehead,
fleas of anxiety drift away; the last
trace of dissonance gone, he looks ahead.

Now he doesn't long for *purvaiya*, the east wind,
or the south wind that travels like a lover from afar,
past lotus and jasmine, smeared with the scents
of the sandalwood groves of distant Malabar.
As she fans him with her palm-leaf pankha,
he notices she has applied sandal paste on her breast,
notices how she un-tousles her hair, which drops
like a black curtain—is she preparing to undress!

She ignores his questioning looks, his agitation,
while cool as a lotus pond she is all poise,
slips off her silver girdle—he knows
that during love she can't stand that noise,

the clink and the clank of it. As she disrobes
he reaches for the pankha, almost wrests
it from her hand and fans her instead,
the sweat-pimpled face, the double-mooned breasts.

THE NIGHT ATTENDANT

The Night Attendant 1

Arms locked, the night sweats
clamber down the back of the shoulders,
move down the spine unnoticed
like moisture from a stalactite,
sheathe the ribs from side to side
and leave them glistening.
They're you, not a part of you,
suddenly they thrust the chill and dry
into chest and lumbar—this is a lesson in anatomy,
not a class on dry and wet.

The Night Attendant 2

The night attendant is here,
so is the night.
But before you think of
ferrying me through murk, or dark
or blanketing colour,
I want you to know some rules:
The scale small, stooping shoulder and low ceiling go together
in harmony here;
nothing big, no argosy with lighted tapers
traversing the skies, no
laser light-sweeps from neighbouring galaxies.
This is just a lit memory, travelling down a road
which happens to be my body, heart, mind,
turning time and its tenses askew,
turning light and dark around; sound to quiet.
Don't reach for light without shadow,
but you are free to ask for fire-glow
without heat or burn or scald,
and for word and lit memory going hand in hand.

The Night Attendant 3

The night attendant is here,
so is the night.
He is in a limbo,
must carry himself through tunnels
locked, interlocked, rusted,
still clasping each other
in airy infructuous embrace;
but he hopes the tunnels may open up
to small slivers of nocturnal light
when he comes to them:
Thresholds always have a little light of their own;
and there are dreams that will cart him,
though he has no idea about them;
can they take his weight?
Will they take his weight?

The Night Attendant 4

A night attendant has no business
dreaming about space.
A dream itself is made of space.
He has no business to dream.
There are walls and he can't open walls,
there are doors and he is frightened: What if
he unlocks them and falls into the night?
The night attendant is as frightened of the night as you are.

The Night Attendant 5

The night attendant said,
'I am not going to run'—
no bravura to his gesture,
just six words dropping like a trickle of sweat
down his chin,
face impassive.
Then he spread his body on the mat
and ran over it
and he ran over his soul,
not knowing it was his soul.

She Said

'I am no good now,
don't wish to hang on any more,
if a street straggles to its end
there's nothing more to it.
No one sees endings,
there are no walls, sorrow lines,
just landscapes outside that shrink into a room.
I have lived with river and sand and breeze,
what else is there to live for?
Sorrow should not be mixed with endings,
a bird will tell you that on its last flight,
though it may not know it is its last flight.'

What is wrong, where are you taking your things?

'Am moving out, don't wish to leave clutter,
a throb of emptiness must linger for a moment
and that's about it, just a throb, a moment,
no entanglements with space.'

Nothing Big

Are you moving out into the night?
Come on, leave large things to themselves.
Treat yourself to the small;
night will not untilt itself for us,
leave Ursa Minor where it is,
glowing like a Christmas tree.
We have flushed out words like
desolation from the room,
have washed away longing, especially for the past.
My silence does not sink into you or into walls,
I am not interested in your dreaming
or un-dreaming;
you want to sleep with your dream on your left,
with me on the right, you've never said this
but I don't want any part of it.
No, I am not going to brood on time.
No large words, please, am done with them.
What if the night attendant runs away with the night?
There will be a skid mark de-dreaming itself.
A hearse driver having his cup of morning chai
at a tea shop may drive up. Am not looking for something big,
just a small erasure.

Goddess on the Grindstone

When the world set off again
In pursuit of what it didn't know it was chasing
the goddess came down and sat on the grindstone,
poured millet down the chute
and swung with her right arm;
closed her ears with her scarf,
didn't like sound, and peering down the hill,
found the white river moving ahead
and looked up and saw the fish owl
shoot off like an arrow (sky itself was the bow),
saw it dodge an air draught, swivel
and align itself to the white river.
She saw a yellow sprig and asked, 'Where did you
spring from?' and found her fingers around the grindstone
turning numb and asked, 'What brought you here?'
But autumn never answered,
too busy with the leaf edge
looking for gold.

List of Illustrations

Page 39: *Neapolitan Lighthouse (1842)* by Ivan Aivazovsky.

Page 53: Alaskan Bald Eagle. Photo by Dave Menke; National Digital Library of the United States Fish and Wildlife Service.

Page 73: 'Abandon all hope, all ye who enter'. One of the illustrations for a French edition of Dante's *The Divine Comedy* by the 19th-century French artist Gustave Doré.

Page 81: The Black Death: A depiction of Death sweeping through crowds and cutting them down during the bubonic plague. Undated; source: Wikimedia Commons.

Page 121: Lunar eclipse. A NASA image.

ALSO FROM SPEAKING TIGER

NAISHAPUR AND BABYLON
Poems (2005-2017)

Keki N. Daruwalla

**Twelve years of poems—vigorous, wise and memorable—
from one of South Asia's finest poets.**

'Over the course of Keki Daruwalla's long career, some things have stayed the same: a vertical view of history that plunges across centuries and mythologies, an epic canvas rendered in minute detail, and a narrative engine that never stops ticking. What has changed is a tonal quality. Early poems that drip with scorn segue into the lovely late lyrics, with their grudging acceptance of mortality and frailty. This is an essential collection, a summing-up, as well as a fount of instruction and pleasure.' —Jeet Thayil

'Daruwalla's verbs have lost none of their feral quality. His poetic line remains, for the most part, sinewy and energetic. The capacity to combine atmospheric sweep with succinctness, and to turn out the startling turn of phrase with an almost throwaway air are unchanged. Several moments in these poems linger long after one has closed the book: the wind "whetting its razor on eroded slopes", "leaves like old scrolls wrapped in their crackling selves", "a firefly pulsing/low on battery", "the tangled reed-and-sedge locks of Shiva", and "elegy moving like a slow Wagnerian movement", to name just a few [...] Vigorous and powerful, the poems of Keki Daruwalla continue to take wing.' —Arundhathi Subramaniam

ALSO FROM SPEAKING TIGER

GOING

Stories of Kinship

Keki N. Daruwalla

'This is a gem of a book...These stories will resonate with all readers. Daruwalla is a consummate storyteller and has the ability to bring characters to life in a few deft strokes.'
—The Tribune

A man drifts away from family and home and becomes a monk, yet nothing fills the void. The only constants are dreams and hallucinations where his mother sometimes appears.

Another son retreats to his room, then disappears. It has been ten years and the father, Sudhakar, doesn't want to harbour false hope, but the mother, Hemlata, clings to it.

Ardeshir and Firoza face a similar predicament. Only their daughter, Arnavaz, hasn't gone missing; she lives with them, even in her absence.

A woman, half-estranged from her mother, comes to visit her grandmother, perhaps for the last time.

'[This] collection explores the nuances of familial ties and their discontents. Poetry seeps into Daruwalla's prose as naturally as rain seeps into the parched earth...Daruwalla weaves the [stories] together to form an exquisite whole.'
—The Hindu